YOU KNOW YOU ARE

A RUNNER...

by Richard McChesney

illustrated by Brighty & Brock

You Know You Are a Runner... is the first book in the "You Know You Are" series.

Other books in the "You Know You Are" series are:

- You Know You Are A Nurse...
- You Know You Are An Engineer...
- You Know You Are A Dog Lover...
- You Know You Are A Golfer...
- You Know You Are Getting Older...
- You Know You Are A Teacher...
- You Know You Are A Mother...

Visit www.YouKnowYouAreBooks.com to join our mailing list and be notified when future titles are released, or find us at www.facebook.com/YouKnowYouAreBooks, or follow us on twitter (@YouKnowYouAreBK)

First edition published 2013 by Strictly Business Limited

Happy reading!

YOU KNOW YOU ARE A RUNNER
WHEN YOUR FAMILY VACATION IS PLANNED
AROUND YOUR NEXT BIG RACE...

YOU KNOW YOU ARE A RUNNER
WHEN YOU HAVE YOUR RUNNING GEAR HANDY
'JUST IN CASE'...

YOU KNOW YOU ARE A RUNNER
WHEN YOU THINK THE SOLUTION TO
ALL THE WORLD'S PROBLEMS IS TO
"GO FOR A RUN"...

YOU KNOW YOU ARE A RUNNER
WHEN YOU GET EXCITED ABOUT SHOE
SHOPPING IN A SPORTS STORE...

YOU KNOW YOU ARE A RUNNER

WHEN AN ESCALATOR IS MORE
USEFUL FOR ACHILLES STRETCHES
THAN REACHING THE NEXT LEVEL...

YOU KNOW YOU ARE A RUNNER
WHEN YOU CAN'T TELL THE DIFFERENCE BETWEEN YOUR CHEST AND YOUR BACK...

YOU KNOW YOU ARE A RUNNER
WHEN YOU CAN'T BEAR TO PART WITH YOUR FAVORITE RUNNING T-SHIRT...

YOU KNOW YOU ARE A RUNNER
WHEN A SUCCESSFUL PIT STOP BEHIND A
BUSH TAKES LESS THAN 60 SECONDS...

YOU KNOW YOU ARE A RUNNER
WHEN YOUR INJURIES ARE PERSONALLY
FUNDING YOUR PHYSIOTHERAPIST'S
NEXT VACATION...

ONE FIRST CLASS TICKET TO
RIO, PLEASE. YEP, THAT'S
RIGHT - MR JONES HAS
SPRAINED HIS ANKLE **AGAIN,**
BRILLIANT, ISNT IT?!!

YOU KNOW YOU ARE A RUNNER
WHEN A BANANA IS NO LONGER JUST
A BANANA...

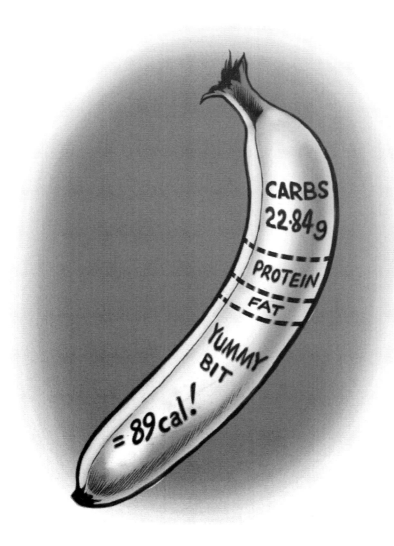

YOU KNOW YOU ARE A RUNNER
WHEN 3 COURSES JUST AREN'T ENOUGH...

YOU KNOW YOU ARE A RUNNER
WHEN YOU EXIT THE WOODS ON A LONG RUN
AND NEED TO ASK WHAT TOWN YOU'RE IN...

YOU KNOW YOU ARE A RUNNER
WHEN YOU CAN'T ATTEND CHURCH BECAUSE
SUNDAY IS 'LONG RUN DAY'...

YOU KNOW YOU ARE A RUNNER

WHEN YOUR FAMILY AND FRIENDS PRETEND
TO UNDERSTAND YOU, BUT REALLY THINK YOU
ARE MAD AND SHOULD BE COMMITTED...

YOU KNOW YOU ARE A RUNNER
WHEN YOUR RIBS CAN BE COUNTED WITHOUT
THE NEED FOR AN X-RAY...

YOU KNOW YOU ARE A RUNNER
WHEN YOUR CLOSET IS OVERFLOWING WITH
RUNNING SHOES, NEW AND OLD...

YOU KNOW YOU ARE A RUNNER
WHEN YOUR EX SAID, "IT'S EITHER ME OR RUNNING", AND YOU'RE NOW SINGLE...

YOU KNOW YOU ARE A RUNNER
WHEN YOU HAVE SPIT HANGING FROM YOUR
CHIN AND YOU DON'T EVEN CARE...

YOU KNOW YOU ARE A RUNNER
WHEN A BIG HILL MAKES YOU
FOAM AT THE MOUTH...

YOU KNOW YOU ARE A RUNNER
WHEN YOU HAVE FORGOTTEN HOW TO PUT ON A BRA WITH HOOKS...

YOU KNOW YOU ARE A RUNNER
WHEN THE DOCTOR FALLS ASLEEP DURING YOUR STRESS TEST...

YOU KNOW YOU ARE A RUNNER

WHEN YOUR WORST NIGHTMARES ARE ARRIVING LATE FOR A RACE OR FORGETTING YOUR RUNNING SHOES...

YOU KNOW YOU ARE A RUNNER
WHEN A 'REST DAY' MAKES YOU AGITATED...

YOU KNOW YOU ARE A RUNNER
WHEN MOWING THE LAWN BECOMES
CROSS TRAINING...

HOW THE HECK DID
I GET HERE?

YOU KNOW YOU ARE A RUNNER
WHEN YOU CAN DRINK WHILE RUNNING WITHOUT SPILLING A DROP...

YOU KNOW YOU ARE A RUNNER
WHEN YOU HAVE CHAFING IN STRANGE AND UNMENTIONABLE PLACES...

YOU KNOW YOU ARE A RUNNER
WHEN YOU GET AN INVITATION TO A WEDDING
AND AUTOMATICALLY THINK ABOUT WHAT RACE
THE DATE WILL CONFLICT WITH...

YOU KNOW YOU ARE A RUNNER
WHEN YOU SPRUCE UP FOR A BIG RACE,
RATHER THAN A BIG DATE...

YOU KNOW YOU ARE A RUNNER
WHEN YOUR RUNNING CLOTHES
DOUBLE AS PJ'S FOR A SPEEDY
GETAWAY IN THE MORNING...

YOU KNOW YOU ARE A RUNNER
WHEN YOU FORGET HOW TO BLOW YOUR NOSE IN PUBLIC...

YOU KNOW YOU ARE A RUNNER
WHEN YOU PURCHASE PINS AND
NEEDLES FOR THE SOLE PURPOSE
OF POPPING BLISTERS...

YOU KNOW YOU ARE A RUNNER
WHEN YOU CAN'T QUITE REMEMBER THEIR NAME, BUT YOU CAN REMEMBER THEIR HIGH SCHOOL MILE TIME...

YOU KNOW YOU ARE A RUNNER
WHEN YOU THINK THAT HALF OF 26.2 IS 20...

YOU KNOW YOU ARE A RUNNER
WHEN YOU WOULD RATHER RUN 10 MILES
THAN TAKE YOUR WIFE OUT FOR DINNER
AND A MOVIE...

YOU KNOW YOU ARE A RUNNER
WHEN YOU CAN'T REMEMBER THE LAST TIME
YOU HAD TEN TOENAILS – ON YOUR FEET...

YOU KNOW YOU ARE A RUNNER

WHEN KEEPING AN EYE ON THE COLOR
OF YOUR PEE IS AS NATURAL AS
CLEANING YOUR TEETH...

YOU KNOW YOU ARE A RUNNER
WHEN PEOPLE REPEATEDLY ASK IF
YOU ARE UNWELL...

YOU KNOW YOU ARE A RUNNER
WHEN YOU ASK TO BE DROPPED OFF HALF
WAY HOME FROM A PARTY SO THAT YOU
CAN RUN THE REST OF THE WAY...

YOU KNOW YOU ARE A RUNNER
WHEN YOU TRY TO IMPRESS WITH THE LINE, "I'M A FAST FINISHER!"...

So... are you a
runner?

You have just read the first book in the "You Know You Are" series.

Other "You Know You Are" books are:

- You Know You Are A Nurse...
- You Know You Are An Engineer...
- You Know You Are A Dog Lover...
- You Know You Are A Golfer...
- You Know You Are Getting Older...
- You Know You Are A Teacher...
- You Know You Are A Mother...

If you enjoyed this book why not join our mailing list to be notified when future titles are released – visit www.YouKnowYouAreBooks.com, or find us on facebook (www.facebook.com/YouKnowYouAreBooks), or follow us on twitter (@YouKnowYouAreBK)

Special thanks to the illustrators who made this book possible:

- **Brighty**
  Cover and Pages 1, 3, 6, 8, 10, 13, 15, 16, 18, 20, 22, 25, 26, 28, 31, 34, 35, 36, 38, 39
- **Brock**
  Pages 2, 4, 5, 7, 9, 11, 12, 14, 17, 19, 21, 23, 24, 27, 29, 30, 32, 33, 37, 40

Other 'You Know You Are' books include:

Visit www.YouKnowYouAreBooks.com for further details.

15026350R00051

Made in the USA
San Bernardino, CA
11 September 2014